Engineering

Engineering

Edited by Raina G. Merchant

Britannica®
Educational Publishing

IN ASSOCIATION WITH

ROSEN
EDUCATIONAL SERVICES

Published in 2017 by Britannica Educational Publishing (a trademark of Encyclopædia Britannica, Inc.) in association with The Rosen Publishing Group, Inc.
29 East 21st Street, New York, NY 10010

Distributed exclusively by Rosen Publishing.
To see additional Britannica Educational Publishing titles, go to rosenpublishing.com.

First Edition

Britannica Educational Publishing
J.E. Luebering: Director, Core Reference Group
Anthony L. Green: Editor, Compton's by Britannica

Rosen Publishing
Raina G. Merchant: Editor
Nelson Sá: Art Director
Brian Garvey: Designer
Cindy Reiman: Photography Manager

Library of Congress Cataloging-in-Publication Data

Engineering / Edited by Raina G. Merchant. — First Edition.
    pages cm. — (The study of science)
 Includes index.
 ISBN 978-1-68048-238-6 (library bound)
 1. Engineering—Juvenile literature. I. Merchant, Raina G., editor.
 TA149.E53 2015
 620 — dc23
                            2015021276

Manufactured in China

CONTENTS

CONTENTS

Early civil engineers applied the principles of military engineering to civilian projects to design and build such structures as bridges. The Clifton Suspension Bridge, seen here, spans the Avon Gorge in England. It was opened in 1864.

The engineer is both related to and separate from the scientist. At its heart, engineering involves applying scientific principles to natural resources in order to design, develop, or improve structures, machines, devices, manufacturing processes, or some combination thereof in order to benefit humankind. Engineers may also be tasked with anticipating how structures, machines, or manufacturing processes might operate under varying conditions.

The words *engine* and *ingenious* are derived from the same Latin root, *ingenerare*, which means "to create." The early English verb *engine* meant "to contrive." The engines of war were devices such as

catapults, floating bridges, and assault towers; their designer was the "engine-er," or military engineer. The counterpart of the military engineer was the civil engineer, who applied essentially the same knowledge and skills to designing buildings, streets, water supplies, sewage systems, and other projects.

Associated with engineering is a great body of special knowledge. Preparation for the practice of engineering involves extensive training in the application of that knowledge. Standards of engineering practice are maintained through the efforts of professional societies, usually organized on a national or regional basis, with each member acknowledging a responsibility to the public over and above responsibilities to his or her employer or to other members of society.

The function of the scientist is to know, while that of the engineer is to do. The scientist adds to the store of knowledge of the physical world; the engineer applies this knowledge to practical problems. Engineering is based principally on physics, chemistry, and mathematics and their extensions into materials science, thermodynamics, and other fields of knowledge.

Unlike the scientist, the engineer is not free to select the problem that he or she finds interesting; engineers must solve problems as they arise, and their solutions must satisfy conflicting requirements. For example, making something more efficient may increase the cost of building it; adding safety measures to a design may increase its complexity. The challenge to the engineer is finding the optimum solution—the end result that, taking many factors into account, is most desirable.

Engineers employ two types of natural resources—materials and energy. Materials are useful because of their physical and chemical properties: strength, ease of production, durability, and the ability to insulate or conduct are just a few examples of critical properties. Important energy sources include fossil fuels (coal, petroleum, gas), wind, sunlight, falling water, and nuclear fission. Since most resources are limited, the engineer must be concerned with the continual development of new resources as well as the efficient utilization of existing ones.

The achievements of engineering are wide-ranging. Engineers have been responsible for some of history's greatest achievements, including the Pyramids of Giza, the Colosseum in Rome, and the Great Wall of China, among countless other structures. Engineering has also made modern society possible. It has

increased the human life span and allowed for healthier living. It has added to leisure time and reduced the long hours of work. Engineering technology can allow the world to feed itself. It has already reduced the negative effects of natural catastrophes such as famines and floods. The world is now a smaller place where people can readily communicate with each other and travel rapidly anywhere. Engineering has raised the standard of living, at least in the developed nations, to a point unimaginable only a century ago. The foundations of this constantly evolving field and the many subfields that comprise it are examined in the following pages.

CHAPTER 1

ENGINEERING FIELDS

Broadly defined, engineering is the science-based profession by which the physical forces of nature and the properties of matter are made useful to humans in the form of structures, machines, and other products or processes at a reasonable expenditure of time and money. An engineer conceives, designs, creates, and implements apparatuses or processes to solve economic, environmental, or social problems. Engineering also is used to create or improve end products. As a problem-solving profession, engineering requires the application of mathematical, scientific, and technical principles.

The various branches of engineering serve a wide range of industries. Electrical engineers, for example, design communications equipment, electric power plants, and computers and other electrical devices. Mechanical engineers deal with machines such as engines and motors, as well as with manufacturing such equipment. An

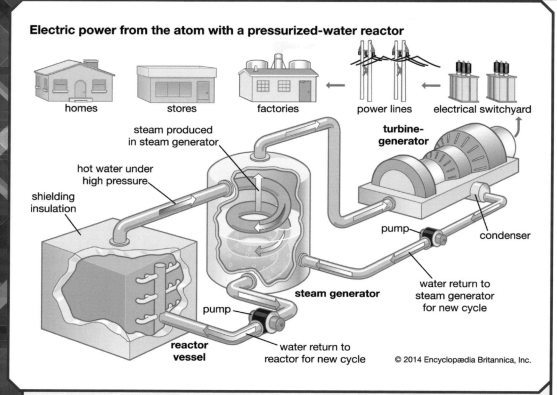

Electric power from the atom with a pressurized-water reactor

homes | stores | factories | power lines | electrical switchyard

steam produced in steam generator

turbine-generator

hot water under high pressure

shielding insulation

pump

condenser

steam generator

water return to steam generator for new cycle

pump

reactor vessel

water return to reactor for new cycle

© 2014 Encyclopædia Britannica, Inc.

A nuclear power plant resembles a conventional power plant, except that a nuclear reactor replaces the steam boiler. An engineer working in such a plant must know about multiple engineering fields.

engineer working in one specialty usually requires some knowledge in associated fields, as most engineering problems are complex and interrelated. A mechanical engineer designing a power plant, for instance, must deal with materials, structures, and electrical equipment in addition to problems related purely to mechanical engineering. Major industrial work very often requires the talents of many engineers with different technical backgrounds and expertise.

The variety of activities in the field furthermore demands people with different levels of education and experience. Engineering encompasses the activities of professional engineers, engineering technologists, and technicians. Whereas engineers deal with the advanced areas in which the latest tools of technology are required, tasks that require only well-established approaches may be performed by technologists. Technologists also play a key role in implementing engineering activities. Technicians normally perform more practical work in the shop or in the laboratory while following well-defined procedures.

Engineering may be divided into a number of major traditional branches. The largest are electrical, mechanical, civil, industrial, and chemical engineering. There also exist several specialized areas that may be characterized as subfields of the major branches.

AEROSPACE ENGINEERING

The design, modeling, development, manufacture, maintenance, testing, analysis, and use of aircraft, spacecraft, satellites, rockets, and

missiles is the work of aerospace engineers. Engineers who work with aircraft are sometimes called aeronautical engineers, while those who work with spacecraft may be called astronautical engineers. The field requires knowledge of aerodynamics, structural design, propulsion equipment, controls, and electronic communications, or avionics. Astronautical engineers must also have a background in rocket propulsion and space navigation.

BIOENGINEERING

A relatively new field, bioengineering (also called biomedical engineering) applies engineering principles to solve medical and biological problems. Uniting engineering and medicine, bioengineers work closely with medical personnel such as physicians, nurses, therapists, and medical technicians to design and construct medical instruments and advanced equipment used in modern hospitals. Bioengineers design artificial limbs, artificial hearts, and other organ substitutes. They conduct fundamental research to solve clinical problems, such as the prevention, diagnosis, and treatment of diseases. In another direction, the bioengineer may use engineering methods to achieve biosynthesis of animal

Bioengineers draw on knowledge of mechanical engineering, biology, and medicine to design artificial limbs, such as this artificial forearm.

or plant products—such as for fermentation processes. Bioengineers must have a background in the biological sciences in addition to engineering.

CHEMICAL ENGINEERING

An especially diverse profession, chemical engineering deals with the large-scale production or conversion of chemicals for industrial use. Problems are usually divided into unit operations or unit processes such as distillation,

17

evaporation, separation of constituent materials, mixing, and so forth. Knowledge of chemical reactions and of the basic laws of conservation of matter and energy is critical to the understanding of most unit processes. The chemical engineer must be able to move from the laboratory to large-scale and economical industrial production by arranging all the unit operations in their proper sequence. Rather than processing a single batch of material at a time, continuous production is used in many modern plants for efficient operation.

Chemical engineers must apply principles of chemistry, physics, mathematics, and materials science, as well as of mechanical and electrical engineering. The duties of a chemical engineer overlap many fields.

CIVIL ENGINEERING

One of the oldest of the engineering fields is civil engineering, which is concerned with structural works. It is very broad with many subspecialties, including structural, geotechnical, water resource, and transportation engineering. Structural engineers are concerned with the safe design and construction of structures. These can range from small warehouses to skyscrapers, from highway

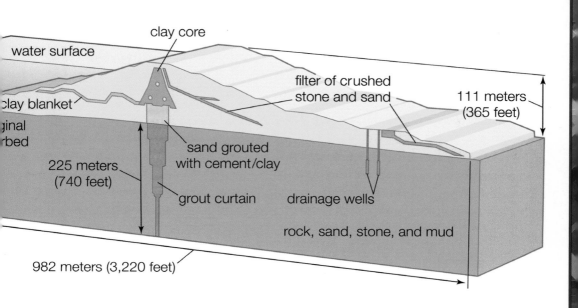

clay core

water surface

filter of crushed
stone and sand

111 meters
(365 feet)

clay blanket

ginal
rbed

225 meters
(740 feet)

sand grouted
with cement/clay

grout curtain

drainage wells

rock, sand, stone, and mud

982 meters (3,220 feet)

This diagram of the Aswan High Dam in Egypt illustrates some of the numerous factors water resource engineers would have to consider when designing such a structure.

overpasses to large bridges, and can include dams of all sizes. Geotechnical and soil mechanics engineers evaluate the capacity of rocks and soils to bear heavy structures. Water resource engineers handle water collection, distribution, and purification, including the building of dams, flood control, and irrigation. Transportation engineers design highway and public transportation systems.

MILITARY ENGINEERING

Military engineering is the oldest of the engineering skills and was the precursor of the profession of civil engineering. The term *civil engineering* was first used in the 18th century to distinguish the newly recognized profession from military engineering, which until then had been the dominant practice.

Modern military engineering can be divided into three main tasks: (1) combat engineering, or tactical engineer support on the battlefield; (2) strategic support through work and services needed in communications zones, such as airfield construction, the improvement of ports, roads, and rail communications, and the storage and distribution of fuels; and (3) ancillary support, such as the provision and distribution of maps and the disposal of unexploded bombs, mines, and other warheads. Construction, fortification, camouflage, demolition, surveying, and mapping are the province of military engineers. They build bases, airfields, depots, roads, bridges, port facilities, and hospitals. In peacetime military engineers also carry out a wide variety of civil-works programs.

COMPUTER ENGINEERING

A subspecialty that combines electrical engineering with computer science, computer engineering concerns all aspects of computer systems, including the design, construction, implementation, and operation of hardware and software for personal and business computers. Some computer engineers specialize in areas such as digital systems, operating systems, computer networks, computer-aided design, and robotics. Computer engineers must possess a foundation in physics and mathematics as well as in electronics, programming, operating systems, data communications, and other related subjects.

ELECTRICAL AND ELECTRONIC ENGINEERING

The field of electrical engineering began with the production, distribution, and utilization of electric power. The design and manufacture of generators, motors, transmission systems, and their controls are all part of electric power engineering. With the invention of the vacuum tube in the early 20th century, electrical engineering branched into communications systems—including radio and television—or electronic engineering. The complex systems required to switch telephone calls and transmit data through satellite and optical fiber networks are responsibilities of communications engineers. Electric circuits, electronics, logic and

switching, electrical machines, and communications systems are just a few areas with which the electrical engineer must be conversant.

ENVIRONMENTAL ENGINEERING

Environmental engineers are concerned with the safe and environmentally sound disposal and treatment of residential and industrial wastes and the protection of air and water quality. Climate change, automobile emissions, ozone depletion, acid rain, sustainable development, and alternative energy sources are all areas of concern to these engineers. Environmental engineering is an interdisciplinary field that combines civil, chemical, and mechanical engineering and requires the application of biological and chemical principles.

GEOLOGICAL AND MINING ENGINEERING

The fields of geological and mining engineering are concerned with the application of geological knowledge to engineering problems. Geological engineers (also called geoengineers) may work on projects involving reservoir design and location, determining the stability of land (especially slopes) for construction purposes, or assessing earthquake, flood, or subsidence danger in areas considered for roads, pipelines, or other engineering works. Knowledge of soil and rock mechanics, hydrology, and geological principles are essential for the geoengineer.

Mining engineering deals with the discovery and exploration of mineral deposits, the various processes to extract these minerals, and their conversion into useful metals or other refined products. Mining engineers are responsible for the safe, economical, and environmentally sound operation of coal, metal, and mineral mines. Petroleum engineering, a subspecialty of this field, concerns the discovery of oil and gas sites and the economic recovery of these fuels. An understanding of geology, rock mechanics, extraction processes, and the behavior of ores and metals is required.

GENETIC ENGINEERING

Genetic engineering is the artificial manipulation, modification, and recombination of DNA or other nucleic acid molecules in order to modify an organism or a population of organisms. The term *genetic engineering* initially encompassed all of the methods used

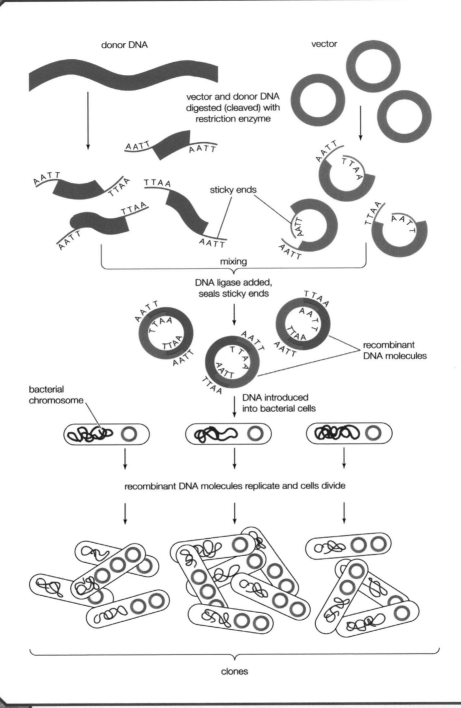

donor DNA

vector

vector and donor DNA
digested (cleaved) with
restriction enzyme

AATT

AATT

AATT

TTAA

TTAA

TTAA

AATT

AATT

TTAA

AATT

AATT

TTAA

AATT

sticky ends

AATT

AATT

AATT

mixing

DNA ligase added,
seals sticky ends

AATT

TTAA

TTAA

AATT

AATT

TTAA

AATT

TTAA

AATT

TTAA

AATT

AATT

TTAA

recombinant
DNA molecules

bacterial
chromosome

DNA introduced
into bacterial cells

recombinant DNA molecules replicate and cells divide

clones

This diagram illustrates the steps involved in the engineering of a recombinant DNA molecule. DNA molecules from two different species are joined together and inserted into a host organism to produce new genetic combinations.

for modifying organisms through heredity and reproduction. These included selective breeding, or artificial selection, as well as a wide range of biomedical techniques such as artificial insemination, in vitro fertilization, and gene manipulation. Today, however, the term refers largely to the latter technique, specifically the field of recombinant DNA technology. In this process, DNA molecules from two or more sources are combined and then inserted into a host organism, such as a bacterium. Inside the host cell, the inserted, or foreign, DNA replicates and functions along with the host DNA. Knowledge of genetics, molecular biology, and biochemistry is critical to the genetic engineer.

INDUSTRIAL AND MANAGEMENT ENGINEERING

The efficient use of a modern factory—including the layout of machines, the best use of human labor, and the safe operation of the plant—fall into the domain of industrial engineers. They are also involved in quality control and inspection to check that the final products meet specifications. Production techniques, automation, statistics, operations research, and the interaction between humans and

Industrial engineers ensure that machines such as this that operate as part of assembly line production in factories continue to function as efficiently as possible.

machines (ergonomics) are some of the fields that must be mastered by the industrial engineer. Management engineering is an extension that adds the role of management to complex technical processes.

MATERIALS ENGINEERING

The study and development of appropriate materials to meet various industrial needs is involved in materials engineering. If the emphasis is on metals, the term *metallurgical engineer* is generally applied. Materials engineering also covers the development of plastics (polymers), ceramics, semiconductors, and composite materials. Materials engineers investigate the properties and behavior of materials and apply principles of chemistry, mathematics, and physics to arrive at the best material solution to a particular problem. Often materials engineers work not forward but backward, to determine the particular reasons a material in service did not perform as expected.

MECHANICAL ENGINEERING

Mechanical engineering encompasses the design, construction, and utilization of machines. These may be involved in the conversion of energy such as in the production of useful work from fuels. Automotive engines, gas turbines, and steam power plants fall into this category. The conversion of fluid and mechanical power in pumps, fans, propellers, and hydraulic turbines is another aspect of mechanical engineering.

Mechanical engineers also design machine components, such as the transmission, steering system, and brakes of a car. Mechanical design can involve large machines, such as presses or forges, or complex equipment such as textile machinery. Frequently it deals with the design of machines used to make other machines—the so-called machine tools, including computer-controlled lathes and milling machines. Design and production of air conditioning, refrigeration, and ventilation systems, and the control of air pollution, also fall into mechanical engineering, as does manufacturing engineering, or the making of parts

Computer-controlled lathes, such as the one seen here, can precisely design intricate parts of other machines. Mechanical engineers are responsible for the design of these and other machines.

and components (sometimes with the help of robots). The mechanical engineer must have knowledge of thermodynamics, fluid mechanics, heat transfer, machine design, vibrations, controls, and robotics.

Nuclear Engineering

The safe design and operation of nuclear power plants are the responsibilities of nuclear engineers. These engineers are concerned with shielding systems to safeguard people from the harmful effects of radiation and with the safe disposal of nuclear wastes. In addition to requiring a knowledge of nuclear physics, the field involves an understanding of materials that can withstand high temperatures and bombardment by nuclear particles as well as many aspects of mechanical engineering.

CHAPTER 2

ENGINEERING FUNCTIONS AND EDUCATION

Problem solving is common to all engineering work. The problem may involve quantitative or qualitative factors; it may be physical or economic; it may require abstract mathematics or common sense. Of great importance is the process of creative synthesis or design, putting ideas together to create a new and optimum solution.

Although engineering problems vary in scope and complexity, the same general approach applies in the various subfields. First comes an analysis of the situation and a preliminary decision on a plan of attack. In line with this plan, the problem is reduced to a more specific question that can be clearly stated. The stated question is then answered by deductive reasoning, an approach that uses logic to move from a general to a specific point. The answer or design is always checked for accuracy and adequacy. Finally, the results for the simplified problem are interpreted in terms of the

original problem and reported appropriately. Engineering education programs offer specialized training in the different subfields, but to varying degrees, and prepare students in the major functions and skills common to all.

FUNCTIONS OF ENGINEERING

Many engineers are employed in industry, working in large manufacturing organizations. Their jobs differ significantly in such areas as design, construction, operations, and maintenance. The functions of the main areas of engineering are described in the sections that follow.

RESEARCH

The research engineer tries to develop new principles and processes by using mathematics, scientific concepts, and experimentation. For instance, large computer simulations developed by research engineers permit the prediction of the performance of an airplane to the point that wind-tunnel and flight testing have been significantly reduced. Most research engineers hold advanced degrees, usually doctorates.

Computer engineers often rely on modeling software to help them design industrial parts. For example, this engineer is designing industrial clutches.

DEVELOPMENT

The development of complex engineering systems requires long periods of time. The process involves component design, often using new materials or new ideas, testing these components, and then improving the original ideas. All of the components must then be put together to build the final engineering system. This often means that the small-scale experiments performed by the researcher must be scaled upward to the level of industrial practice. The chemical engineer, for instance, must extend the findings of a laboratory experiment to a small pilot plant and, if successful, to full-scale production. Engineers engaged in development usually hold advanced degrees.

DESIGN

Coupled with and following development is design. An engineering project must not only work, but it must be safe, economical, and reliable and must meet the needs of the customer. The specific layout of an engineering product or structure becomes the responsibility of the design engineer.

TESTING

Most engineering products must be fully tested before they can be delivered to a customer. Testing may show possible failures. The product then requires redesigning. Development, design, and testing must work closely together.

MANUFACTURING OR CONSTRUCTION

The actual making of parts, whether in a factory or by assembling a structure on-site, involves all the tools of production. The manufacturing

Engineers must test all products to help ensure that all defects or failures are fixed before the products become available to consumers or clients.

engineer selects the right tools, schedules the flow of material and parts for the right machines, and supervises assembly.

QUALITY CONTROL AND INSPECTION

The quality control engineer checks that all raw materials, parts, assemblies, and products meet technical and various other requirements. Quality control engineers monitor and test the quality and safety of products throughout all stages of the manufacturing process.

SALES AND MARKETING

Interaction between the manufacturer and the customer is the responsibility of sales or marketing engineers. Frequently they may need to educate the customers. Engineers specializing in sales and marketing must understand all the technical aspects of their products as well as the needs of their customers. These needs may require the addition of special features or even major redesign of a product. Thus the sales engineer must be in contact with all parts of the manufacturing organization.

Maintenance and operations engineers regularly inspect equipment to ensure that it functions efficiently or that malfunctioning parts are repaired. Here, a turbine is inspected to ensure it continues to function after a power outage.

MAINTENANCE AND OPERATION

The continued safe and reliable operation of equipment and efficient repairs is the responsibility of the maintenance engineer. The operating engineer controls machines, plants, and organizations providing power, transportation, and communication; determines procedures; and supervises personnel to obtain reliable and economic operation of complex equipment. Maintenance and operations usually go hand in hand.

MANAGEMENT

The management of a complex technical venture is different from normal business management. It requires knowledge of both engineering and of management techniques. Most engineering managers are promoted from the ranks of engineers. Often these engineers have advanced training in business administration. In some countries and industries, engineers analyze customers' requirements, recommend units to satisfy needs economically, and resolve related problems.

ENGINEERING TRAINING

Until the 18th century, engineering was essentially a craft in which cumulative experience was considered more important than formal learning. The exception was military engineering, in which formal education dates back to the middle of the 17th century. Education in civil engineering began in 1747 with the founding in France of the National School of Bridges and Highways. France influenced the United States: the first American school of engineering was the United States Military Academy at West Point, N.Y., founded in 1802. It operated

Before becoming the "father of the military academy," Sylvanus Thayer was a member of the U.S. Army Corps of Engineers.

under the leadership of Sylvanus Thayer. Several two-year schools were founded before 1830 that emphasized technical education. Some of these eventually evolved into engineering colleges. The oldest are Norwich University in Vermont (1819) and the Rensselaer Institute of Technology in Troy, N.Y. (1824). American engineering education did not grow much, however, until after the Civil War, when state universities were founded with federal land grants to teach agriculture and "the mechanic arts."

Such practical crafts courses as machine shop, surveying, drafting, and welding were offered in almost all schools. Although mathematics and the physical sciences were incorporated into engineering education early on, the development of engineering courses based on science and scientific principles began only after 1950.

UNDERGRADUATE

At the university level, engineering is a challenging course of study that requires a thorough understanding of mathematics and science. These subjects are normally taken in the first two years of study. Humanities and social studies also form a part of engineering programs. Such courses are included because engineers must consider the social effects of the products and processes they devise. Good oral and written communication skills also are needed. The last two years of the undergraduate curriculum are devoted almost entirely to technical courses.

More than 360 schools in the United States have one or more engineering programs accredited by the Accrediting Board for Engineering and Technology (ABET). There are also nonaccredited programs, but graduation from a nonaccredited program may make the student ineligible for a professional engineering license in some states or bar employment by federal agencies.

Accreditation in Canada is carried out by the Canadian Accrediting Board of the Canadian Council of Professional Engineers. Programs in more than thirty-five colleges and universities are accredited.

ENGINEERING AT WEST POINT

The United States Military Academy, also called West Point Academy, is an institution of higher education for the training of commissioned officers for the U.S. Army. It was originally founded as a school for the U.S. Corps of Engineers and is one of the oldest service academies in the world. The founding of an American military school had been proposed by General Henry Knox in 1776, and George Washington and Alexander Hamilton had repeatedly urged adoption of the plan, but it was not until March 16, 1802, that Congress passed the act establishing the United States Military Academy at West Point. The academy opened on July 4, 1802. Before 1812 it was conducted as an apprentice school for military engineers and, in effect, as the first U.S. school of engineering. During its early years, however, the institution suffered from lack of proper organization and discipline.

An act of Congress of April 29, 1812, reorganized the academy and increased the authorized strength of the corps of cadets to 250, expanded the staff of the academy, and established a four-year curriculum. This legislative goal was not effective until the superintendency of Colonel Sylvanus Thayer (1817–33), who became known as the "father of the military academy" because of his lasting influence upon the West Point physical plant, the library, the curriculum, and the learning methods. Under Thayer's leadership the academy produced military technicians whose skills were adaptable to meet the civil-engineering needs for the program of internal improvement that accompanied America's westward expansion. An act of Congress of July 13, 1866, allowed the selection of a military academy superintendent from branches of the army other than the Corps of Engineers.

Many students begin their engineering careers right after graduation, while others go on to graduate study. Some students undertake graduate work part-time while employed as engineers. Other graduates use their engineering education to enter a variety of fields, including business administration, medicine, and law.

GRADUATE

With the continuing and rapid changes in technology, it is difficult to teach enough engineering in a four-year undergraduate curriculum. Both master's and doctoral programs stress further technical depth. Doctoral programs require an independent research program resulting in a thesis. Engineers planning to enter management frequently also undertake advanced study in business administration.

CONTINUING EDUCATION

Engineers can quickly become obsolete unless they engage in lifelong learning in the profession. For example, electrical engineers who graduated in the early 1950s would not know about transistors or computers unless they learned about them after leaving college.

Engineers keep their skills and knowledge current through continuing education courses offered by universities, professional societies, and other groups. In some areas, continuing education credits are required in order to renew a professional engineering license.

PROFESSIONAL SOCIETIES

To remain current in their field, most engineers join one or more professional engineering societies. These societies publish technical journals, encourage engineering research, provide assistance to governments, hold meetings at which technical advances are presented, offer continuing education courses, and look after the technical welfare of their members.

One of the earliest civil engineering societies formed was the Institution of Civil Engineers (ICE), established in the United

The Institution of Civil Engineers, founded in 1818, continues to offer professional services to members in the civil engineering industry.

Kingdom in 1818. Some of the major U.S. societies date to the late 1800s: the American Society of Civil Engineers (ACSE) was founded in 1852; the American Institute of Mining, Metallurgical, and Petroleum Engineers (AIME) in 1871; the American Society of Mechanical Engineers (ASME) in 1880; and the forerunner of the Institute of Electrical and Electronics Engineers (IEEE) in 1884. The organization that later became the Engineering Institute of Canada (EIC), now a federation of Canadian engineering societies, was established in 1887.

A myriad of professional societies for engineers in all specialties were founded in the 20th century, including the American Institute of Chemical Engineers (AIChE), the Institute of Industrial Engineers (IIE), the American Nuclear Society (ANS), the American Institute of Aeronautics and Astronautics (AIAA), and the Biomedical Engineering Society (BMES), in the United States; Engineers Australia; and the Institution of Engineers (IEI) in India. The World Federation of Engineering Organizations (WFEO) of the United Nations is an international umbrella organization of professional societies in the field.

CHAPTER 3

THE EARLY HISTORY OF ENGINEERING

The first engineer known by name and achievement was Imhotep, builder of the Step Pyramid at Ṣaqqārah, Egypt, probably in about 2550 BCE. Imhotep's successors—Egyptian, Persian, Greek, and Roman—carried civil engineering to remarkable heights using empirical methods (methods based on observation and evidence) aided by arithmetic, geometry, and a smattering of physical science. The Pharos (lighthouse) of Alexandria, Solomon's Temple in Jerusalem, the Colosseum in Rome, the Persian and Roman road systems, the Pont du Gard aqueduct in France, and many other large structures, some of which endure to this day, testify to the skill, imagination, and daring of these early engineers. Of many treatises written by them, one in particular survives to provide a picture of engineering education and practice in classical times: Vitruvius' *De architectura*, published in Rome in the 1st century CE, a ten-volume

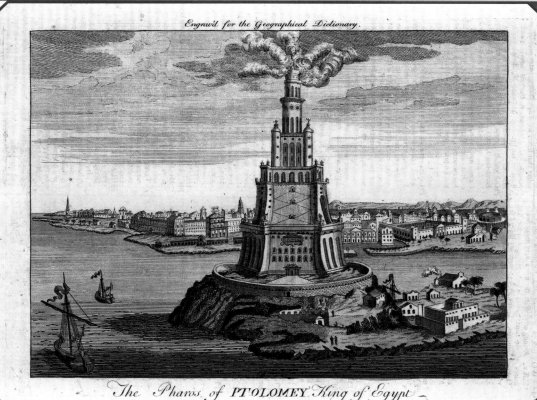

Engrav'd for the Geographical Dictionary.

The Pharos of PTOLOMEY King of Egypt —

The Pharos of Alexandria is considered one of the Seven Wonders of the World for its technological triumphs. At 350 feet (110 meters), the only taller man-made structures at the time were the pyramids of Giza.

work covering building materials, construction methods, hydraulics, measurement, and town planning.

In their methods of construction, medieval European engineers carried technique, in the form of the Gothic arch and flying buttress (light structures of stone piers and arches standing outside the mass of the building

itself) to a height unknown to the Romans. The sketchbook of the 13th-century French engineer Villard de Honnecourt reveals a wide knowledge of mathematics, geometry, natural and physical science, and draftsmanship.

In Asia, engineering had a separate but very similar development, with increasingly sophisticated techniques of construction, hydraulics, and metallurgy helping to create advanced civilizations such as the Mongol Empire, whose large, beautiful cities impressed Marco Polo in the 13th century.

The building of canals, bridges, and roads was carried out by specially trained civil engineers as early as the middle of the 18th century. Civil engineering emerged as a separate discipline in the 18th century, when the first professional societies and schools of engineering were founded. Civil engineers of the 19th century built structures of all kinds, designed water-supply and sanitation systems, laid out railroad and highway networks, and planned cities.

England and Scotland were the birthplace of mechanical engineering, as a derivation of the inventions of the Scottish engineer James Watt and the textile machinists of the Industrial Revolution. The automatic knitting machine was probably the most advanced technology of the day. Originally steam was used merely to extend power beyond that of animals. During the 19th century, however, mechanical engineering expanded to include such labor-saving devices as the sewing machine and the mechanical reaper. The development of the British machine-tool industry gave tremendous impetus to the study of mechanical engineering both in Britain and abroad.

The invention of electric generators and motors and the development of the electric lightbulb led to the growth of electrical engineering, which was originally a subspecialty

A woman works at the spinning machines in a textile mill in Winchendon, Mass., around the turn of the 20th century. The widespread use of such machines led to a rise in the number of mechanical engineers.

of mechanical engineering. The growth of knowledge of electricity—from Alessandro Volta's original electric cell of 1800 through the experiments of Michael Faraday and others, culminating in 1872 in Z.T. Gramme's development of the Gramme dynamo (a continuous-current electrical generator)—helped establish the fields of electrical and electronics engineering. The electronics aspect became prominent through the work of such scientists as James Clerk Maxwell of Britain and Heinrich Hertz of Germany in the late 19th century. Major advances came with the development of the vacuum tube by Lee De Forest of the United States in the early 20th century and the invention of the transistor in the mid-20th century. In the late 20th century electrical and electronics engineers dominated the field of engineering worldwide.

The increasing need for metals furthered mining engineering. With the invention of the Bessemer steel-making process, steel began to replace iron in both machinery and construction. Large bridges and skyscrapers became possible. This led to the development of metallurgical engineering as a separate field. Chemical engineering grew out of the 19th-century proliferation of industrial processes involving chemical reactions in metallurgy, food, textiles, and many other areas. By 1880 the use of chemicals in manufacturing had created an industry whose function was the mass production of chemicals.

The emergence of these fields of engineering, all established to varying degrees by the early 20th century, are examined in greater detail in the sections that follow.

Civil Engineering

The beginnings of civil engineering as a separate discipline may be seen in the founding of the Bridge and Highway Corps in France in 1716. Out of this in 1747 grew the École Nationale des Ponts et Chaussées ("National School of Bridges and Highways"). Its teachers wrote books that became standard works on the mechanics of materials, machines, and hydraulics. So vital were these texts that leading British engineers learned French to read them. As design and calculation replaced rule-of-thumb and empirical formulas, and as expert knowledge was formulated, the non-military engineer moved to the front of the field. Talented, if often self-taught, craftsmen, stonemasons, millwrights, toolmakers, and instrument makers became civil engineers. In Britain, James Brindley began as a millwright

Workers construct the New London Bridge in *c.* 1827, according to the design of civil engineer John Rennie. Though untrained, Rennie also worked on numerous canals, docks, and harbors in England.

and became the foremost canal builder of the century; John Rennie was a millwright's apprentice who eventually built the new London Bridge; Thomas Telford, a stonemason, became Britain's leading road builder.

John Smeaton, the first man to refer to himself as a civil engineer, began as an instrument maker. His design of Eddystone Lighthouse (1756–59), with its interlocking masonry, was based on a craftsman's experience. Smeaton's work was backed by thorough research, and his services were much in demand. In 1771 he founded the Society of Civil Engineers (now known as the Smeatonian Society). Its objective was to bring together experienced engineers, entrepreneurs, and lawyers to promote the building of large public works, such as canals (and later railways), and to secure the parliamentary powers necessary to execute their schemes. Their meetings were held during parliamentary sessions; the society follows this custom to this day.

Two prominent schools of civil engineering were the École Polytechnique, founded in Paris in 1794, and the Bauakademie, started in Berlin in 1799. No such schools existed in Great Britain for another two decades. It was this lack of opportunity for scientific study and for the exchange of experiences that led a group of young men in 1818 to found the Institution of Civil Engineers. The founders were keen to learn from one another and from their elders. In 1820 they invited Thomas Telford, by then the dean of British civil engineers, to be their first president.

There were similar developments elsewhere. By the mid-19th century, there were civil engineering societies in many European countries and the United States, and the following century produced similar institutions in almost every country in the world.

JOHN SMEATON

John Smeaton was born on June 8, 1724, in Austhorpe, Yorkshire, England. He learned mathematical instrument making in London and then concentrated his studies on canals, harbors, and mills. In 1756–59 he built the third Eddystone Lighthouse (the first one was swept away by waves, and the second one was destroyed by fire). He became the first engineer to use interlocking blocks of portland stone to withstand the pounding waves of the sea. He also used mortar made of limestone and a high proportion of clay, effectively developing the first cement for underwater use. Some of Smeaton's other well-known construction projects were completed in Scotland, including the Forth and Clyde Canal, which opened a waterway between the Atlantic and the North Sea.

Smeaton also helped in the transition from wind-and-water power to steam power. He introduced cast-iron shafts and gearing into windmills and water mills, and designed large atmospheric pumping engines for mines and docks. He also improved the safety of the diving bell, a device used to transport divers from the seafloor to the surface, by fitting an air pump to the bell. Smeaton died on Oct. 28, 1792, in Austhorpe.

The Eddystone Lighthouse was celebrated in folk ballads and seamen's lore. John Smeaton built the third Eddystone Lighthouse.

Formal education in engineering science became widely available as other countries followed the lead of France and Germany. In Great Britain the universities, traditionally seats of classical learning, were reluctant to embrace the new disciplines. University College, London, founded in 1826, provided a broad range of academic studies and offered a course in mechanical philosophy. King's College, London, first taught civil engineering in 1838, and in 1840 Queen Victoria founded the first chair of civil engineering and mechanics at the University of Glasgow, Scotland. Rensselaer Polytechnic Institute, founded in 1824, offered the first courses in civil engineering in the United States. The number of universities throughout the world with engineering faculties, including civil engineering, increased rapidly in the 19th and early 20th centuries. Civil engineering today is taught in universities on every continent.

MECHANICAL ENGINEERING

The invention of the steam engine in the latter part of the 18th century provided a key source of power for the Industrial Revolution and gave an enormous boost to the development of

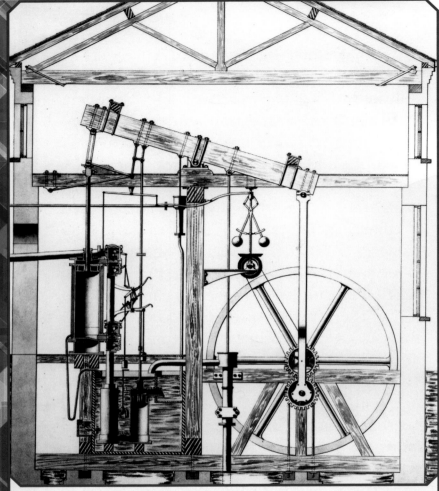

James Watt's original drawing of his rotative steam engine with sun-and-planet gear, 1788, is now in the Science Museum, London. Watt's machine helped launch the Industrial Revolution.

machinery of all types. As a result, mechanical engineering emerged as a new major classification of engineering dealing with tools and machines. The field received formal recognition in 1847 in the founding of

the Institution of Mechanical Engineers in Birmingham, England.

The engineering workshops that matured in the 19th century played a vital part in the increasing mechanization of industry and transport. Not only did they deliver the looms, locomotives, and other hardware in steadily growing quantities, but they also transformed the machine tools on which these machines were made. The lathe became an all-metal, power-driven machine with a completely rigid base and a slide rest to hold the cutting tool, capable of more sustained and vastly more accurate work than the hand- or foot-operated wooden-framed lathes that preceded it. Drilling and slotting machines, milling and planing machines, and a steam hammer invented by James Nasmyth were among the machines devised or improved from earlier woodworking models by the new mechanical engineering industry.

After the middle of the 19th century, specialization within the machinery industry became more pronounced, as some manufacturers concentrated on vehicle production while others devoted themselves to the particular needs of industries such as coal mining, papermaking, and sugar refining. The movement toward greater specialization was accelerated by the establishment of mechanical engineering in

THE STEAM ENGINE

In a steam engine, high-pressure steam is admitted into a reciprocating (back-and-forth) piston-cylinder assembly. As the steam expands to lower pressure, part of the thermal energy is converted into work—the movement of the piston. This movement can be transferred into rotary motion with a crank-crankshaft assembly similar to that used in automobiles. The expanded steam may then be allowed to escape, or, for maximum engine efficiency, the steam may be sent to a separate apparatus—a condenser—at comparatively low temperature and pressure. There the remaining heat is used to warm the water that will be used to make more steam. The steam is usually supplied by a boiler fired with coal, oil, or natural gas.

The earliest steam engines were scientific novelties, such as the aeolipile developed by Hero of Alexandria in the 1st century CE. Not until the 17th century were attempts made to harness steam for practical purposes. In 1698 Thomas Savery patented a pump with hand-operated valves to raise water from mines by suction produced by condensing steam. In about 1712 another Englishman, Thomas Newcomen, developed a more efficient steam engine with a piston separating the condensing steam from the water. In 1765 James Watt greatly improved the Newcomen engine by adding a separate condenser to avoid heating and cooling the cylinder with each stroke. Watt then developed a new engine that rotated a shaft instead of providing the simple up-and-down motion of the pump, and he added many other improvements to produce a practical power plant.

A steam carriage for roads was built in France by Nicholas-Joseph Cugnot as early as 1769. Richard Trevithick in England was the first to use a steam carriage on a railway;

in 1803 he built a steam locomotive that in February 1804 made a successful run on a horsecar route in Wales. The adaptation of the steam engine to railways became a commercial success with the Rocket of English engineer George Stephenson in 1829.

Steam engines improved transport by water as well. The first practical steamboat was the tug *Charlotte Dundas*, built by William Symington and tried in the Forth and Clyde Canal, Scotland, in 1802. Robert Fulton applied the steam engine to a passenger boat in the United States in 1807.

The invention of the steam engine played a major role in the Industrial Revolution by creating a society less dependent on animal power, waterwheels, and windmills. Since the early 1900s, however, the larger and more efficient steam turbine has replaced most steam engines in large electric-power plants. Steam locomotives have largely been supplanted by more reliable and economical diesel-electric locomotives. Early steam automobiles have been superseded by cars powered by internal-combustion engines. Although steam engines today generally are regarded as museum pieces, interest in them revived in the second half of the 20th century because of increasing air-pollution problems caused by the burning of fossil fuels.

the other industrial nations. This was true especially in Germany, where electrical engineering and other new skills made rapid progress, and in the United States, where labor shortages encouraged the development of standardization and mass-production techniques in fields

as widely separated as agricultural machinery, small arms, typewriters, and sewing machines.

Mechanical engineering has evolved from the practice by the mechanic of an art based largely on trial and error to the application by the professional engineer of the scientific method in research, design, and production. The demand for increased efficiency is continually raising the quality of work expected from a mechanical engineer and requiring a higher degree of education and training.

ELECTRICAL ENGINEERING

Electrical phenomena attracted the attention of European thinkers as early as the 17th century. Beginning as a mathematically oriented science, the field has remained primarily in that form; many ideas are based on mathematical models. The most noteworthy pioneers in electrical engineering include Ludwig Wilhelm Gilbert and Georg Simon Ohm of Germany, Hans Christian Ørsted of Denmark, André-Marie Ampère of France, Alessandro Volta of Italy, Joseph Henry of the United States, and Michael Faraday of England.

Electrical engineering may be said to have emerged as a discipline in 1864 when Scottish physicist James Clerk Maxwell summarized the basic laws of electricity in mathematical form to predict that radiation of electromagnetic energy would occur in a form that later became known as radio waves. In 1887 the German physicist Heinrich Hertz experimentally demonstrated the existence of radio waves.

The first practical application of electricity was the telegraph, invented by Samuel F.B.

Thomas Edison established the first power plant in the United States at Pearl Street, in New York City. The dynamo, or electric generator, which converts mechanical energy to electricity for distribution, is seen here.

Morse in 1837. The need for electrical engineers was not felt until some 40 years later, upon the invention of the telephone (1876) by Alexander Graham Bell and of the incandescent lamp (1878) by Thomas Edison. These devices and Edison's first central generating plant in New York City (1882) created a large demand for workers trained to work with electricity.

The discovery of the "Edison effect," a flow of current through the vacuum of one of his lamps, was the first observation of current in space. Hendrick Antoon Lorentz of the Netherlands predicted the electron theory of electrical charge in 1895, and in 1897 J.J. Thomson of England showed that the Edison-effect current was indeed caused by negatively charged particles (electrons). This led to the work of Guglielmo Marconi of Italy, Lee De Forest of the United States, and many others, which laid the foundations of radio engineering.

CHEMICAL ENGINEERING

Chemical engineering is as old as the process industries. Its heritage dates from the fermentation and evaporation processes operated by early civilizations. Modern chemical engineering emerged with the development of

large-scale, chemical manufacturing operations in the second half of the 19th century.
Throughout its development as an independent discipline, chemical engineering has
been directed toward solving problems of
designing and operating large plants for continuous production.

Manufacture of chemicals in the mid-19th
century consisted of modest craft operations.
Increase in demand, public concern at the
emission of toxic wastes, and competition
between rival processes provided incentives
for greater efficiency. This led to the emergence of combines with resources for larger
operations and caused the transition from a
craft to a science-based industry. The result
was a demand for chemists with knowledge of
manufacturing processes, known as industrial
chemists or chemical technologists.

The term *chemical engineer* was in general
use by about 1900. Despite its emergence in
traditional chemicals manufacturing, it was
through its role in the development of the
petroleum industry that chemical engineering became firmly established as a unique
discipline. The demand for plants capable
of operating physical separation processes
continuously at high levels of efficiency was
a challenge that could not be met by the

traditional chemist or mechanical engineer.

A landmark in the development of chemical engineering was the publication in 1901 of the first textbook on the subject, by George E. Davis, a British chemical consultant. This concentrated on the design of plant items for specific operations. The notion of a processing plant encompassing multiple operations, such as mixing, evaporation, and filtration, and of these operations being essentially similar, led to the concept of unit operations. This was first voiced by the American chemical engineer Arthur D. Little in 1915 and formed the basis for a classification of chemical engineering that dominated the subject for the next 40 years.

AERONAUTICAL ENGINEERING

The roots of aeronautical engineering can be traced to the early days of mechanical engineering, to inventors' concepts, and to the initial studies of aerodynamics, a branch of theoretical physics. The earliest sketches of flight vehicles were drawn by Leonardo da Vinci, who suggested two ideas. The first was an ornithopter, a flying machine using flapping wings to imitate the flight of birds. The

Leonardo da Vinci's sketches of mechanical flying machines anticipated airplanes by nearly 500 years.

second idea was an aerial screw, the predecessor of the helicopter.

Manned flight was first achieved in 1783, in a hot-air balloon designed by the French brothers Joseph-Michel and Jacques-Étienne Montgolfier. Aerodynamics became a factor in balloon flight when a propulsion system was considered for forward movement. Benjamin Franklin was one of the first to propose such an idea, which led to development of

the dirigible. The power-driven balloon was invented by Henri Gifford, a Frenchman, in 1852.

The invention of lighter-than-air vehicles occurred independently of the development of aircraft. The breakthrough in aircraft development came in 1799 when Sir George Cayley, an English baron, drew an airplane incorporating a fixed wing for lift, an empennage (consisting of horizontal and vertical tail surfaces for stability and control), and a separate propulsion system. Because engine development was virtually nonexistent, Cayley turned to gliders, building the first successful one in 1849. Gliding flights established a database for aerodynamics and aircraft design. Otto Lilienthal, a German scientist, recorded more than 2,000 glides in a five-year period, beginning in 1891.

Lilienthal's work was followed by the American aeronaut Octave Chanute, a friend of the American brothers Orville and Wilbur Wright, the fathers of modern manned flight. Following the first sustained flight of a heavier-than-air vehicle in 1903, the Wright brothers refined their design, eventually selling airplanes to the U.S. Army.

CHAPTER 4

ENGINEERING DEVELOPMENTS IN THE 20TH AND 21ST CENTURIES

The engineering subfields that had developed by the early 20th century continued to mature with changing societal demands and technological innovations. Additionally, new specialties began to take shape throughout the 20th century and into the 21st.

Following the introduction of the assembly line by Henry Ford in 1913, the demands of the growing automobile industry led to the specialty of automotive engineering. The rapid spurt of airplane development following World War I preceded the new field of aeronautical engineering. The increasing need for petroleum products to provide fuels for transportation and heating fostered petroleum engineering. With the development of radio just after the turn of the 20th century, electronics engineering—a branch of electrical engineering—was born. Today almost all modern communications techniques depend on the electronics engineer. With the invention of the transistor in 1948, new vistas in communications and computing were opened. The information revolution that arose in the late 20th century added computer engineering as a new specialty.

The advent of nuclear power was reflected in the field of nuclear engineering. Advances in medicine and technology combined with the need to build artificial limbs and organs and to improve medical instrumentation started the field of bioengineering. The need to produce goods cheaply and efficiently became a primary responsibility of the industrial engineer. Following the development of space flight, aersospace

COMPUTER-AIDED ENGINEERING

In industry, computer-aided engineering (CAE) integrates design and manufacturing into a system under the direct control of digital computers. Visualization is an essential feature of CAE and computer-aided design (CAD). An engineer can design a bridge, then use modeling software to display it and study it under different loads. CAE software can translate drawings into the precise specification of the parts of a mechanical system. Computer chips themselves are designed with CAD programs that let an engineer write a specification for part of a chip, simulate its behavior, test it, and then generate layouts for the photolithographic process that puts the circuit on the silicon.

Astronomical sky surveys, weather forecasting, and medical imaging such as magnetic resonance imaging, CAT scans, and DNA analyses create very large collections of data. Scientific computation today uses the same kinds of powerful statistical and pattern-analysis techniques as many business applications.

A trainee of the 1970s learns to make engineering drawings at a drafting table. Engineers now create drawings using CAD (computer-assisted design). Workers often must learn new skills during the course of a career.

(astronautical) engineering was added to aeronautical engineering.

The invention of computers not only created a subspecialty in engineering but also changed the way all engineers work. Many structures, components, and processes are designed, modeled, and tested with the aid of computer programs. For example, computers are used to carry out all the technical computations needed to make a machine part meet performance requirements. This aspect of computer-aided design (CAD) is frequently coupled with computer-aided manufacture (CAM) to produce parts automatically. The use of robots is a major factor in the increasing automation of factories.

Major developments in these or related fields are considered in this section. Most fields continue to evolve rapidly as new information and research comes to light. It can only be guessed what will follow the information revolution that began in the late 20th century and was the hallmark of the early 21st.

PETROLEUM ENGINEERING

The foundations of petroleum engineering were established as geologists explored and mapped the relative locations of oil-producing zones and water zones in California in the the 1890s. The work revealed the potential for applying technology to oil-field development. The American Institute of Mining and Metallurgical Engineers (AIME) established a Technical Committee on Petroleum in 1914. In 1957 the name of the AIME was changed to the American Institute of Mining, Metallurgical, and Petroleum Engineers.

Petroleum technology courses were introduced at the University of Pittsburgh in 1910 and included courses in oil and gas law and industry practices; in 1915 the university granted the first degree in petroleum engineering. Also in 1910 the University of California at Berkeley offered its first courses in petroleum engineering, and in 1915 it established a four-year curriculum in the field. After these pioneering efforts, professional programs spread throughout the United States and other countries.

From 1900 to 1920, petroleum engineering focused on drilling problems and on improving mechanical operations in drilling and well pumping. In the 1920s petroleum engineers sought ways to improve drilling practices and to improve well design. They designed new machines and studied various methodologies of production.

The economic crisis that resulted from abundant discoveries in about 1930, notably in the giant East Texas Field, caused petroleum engineering to focus on entire oil-water-gas reservoir systems rather than on individual wells. This led to the concept of reservoir engineering.

The development of the offshore oil industry in the 1950s was a landmark event and introduced a whole new technology. At first little was known of such matters as wave heights and wave forces. The oceanographer and marine engineer thus joined with the petroleum engineer to initiate design standards. Shallow-water drilling barges evolved into mobile platforms, then into jack-up barges, and finally into semi-submersible and floating drilling ships.

ELECTRONICS ENGINEERING

In 1930 the term *electronics* was introduced to embrace radio and the industrial applications of electron tubes. In this way, electronics engineering was distinguished from traditional electrical engineering. Since 1947, when the transistor was invented by John Bardeen, William H. Brattain, and William B. Shockley,

electronics engineering has been dominated by the applications of such solid-state electronic devices as the transistor, the semiconductor diode, and the integrated circuit.

Early transistors were produced using the element germanium as the semiconductor material, because methods of purifying it appropriately had been developed during and shortly after World War II. During the late 1950s, research on silicon produced material suitable for semiconductors. New devices made of silicon were manufactured from about 1960. Silicon quickly became the preferred raw material for semiconductors: it is more abundant than germanium (and thus less expensive) and retains its semiconducting properties at higher temperatures than does germanium.

By 1960 vacuum tubes were rapidly being supplanted by transistors because the latter had become less expensive, did not burn out in service, and were much smaller and more reliable. Computers employed hundreds of thousands of transistors each. This fact, together with the need for compact, lightweight electronic missile-guidance systems, led to the invention of the integrated circuit.

Until the microprocessor appeared on the scene, computers were essentially discrete

pieces of equipment used primarily for data processing and scientific calculations. They ranged in size from minicomputers, comparable in dimensions to a small filing cabinet, to mainframe systems that could fill a large room. The microprocessor enabled computer engineers to develop microcomputers—systems about the size of a lunch box or smaller but with enough computing power to perform many kinds of business, industrial, and scientific tasks. Such systems made it possible to control a host of small instruments or devices (e.g., numerically controlled lathes and one-armed robotic devices for spot welding) by using standard components programmed to do a specific job.

By the mid-1980s inexpensive microprocessors had stimulated computerization of an enormous variety of consumer products. These included programmable microwave ovens and thermostats, clothes washers and dryers, self-tuning television sets and self-focusing cameras, videocassette recorders and video games, telephones and answering machines, musical instruments, watches, and security systems.

Microelectronics also came to the forefront in business, industry, government, and other sectors. Microprocessor-based equipment proliferated, ranging from automatic teller machines (ATMs) and point-of-sale terminals in retail stores to automated factory assembly systems and office workstations.

Because computers have been a major application for integrated circuits from their beginning, digital integrated circuits have become commonplace. As electronic systems become more complex, it is essential that errors produced by noise be removed; otherwise, the systems may malfunction. The only practical way to assure immunity from noise is to make such a system operate digitally. A consequence of the veritable explosion in the number and kinds of electronic systems has been a sharp growth in the electrical noise level of the environment.

A new direction in electronics employs photons (packets of light) instead of electrons. By common consent these new approaches are included in electronics, because the functions that are performed are, at least for the present, the same as those performed by electronic systems and because these functions usually are embedded in a largely electronic environment.

This new direction is called optical electronics, or optoelectronics.

NUCLEAR ENGINEERING

Nuclear engineering was born in the 20th century with the announcement in 1939 of the discovery of nuclear fission by the German chemists Otto Hahn and Fritz Strassmann. It was almost immediately realized that a weapon of enormous explosive energy might be possible by employing fission. During World War II, the race to be the first to build this weapon led to the creation of the Manhattan Project in the United States. The seminal work of the Manhattan Project, led by Italian physicist Enrico Fermi, was the building of the first nuclear reactor in 1942 at the University of Chicago. Named Chicago Pile No. 1 (CP-1), this reactor demonstrated the scientific theory of a controlled nuclear chain reaction.

Development of CP-1 was followed by the construction of reactors at Hanford, Washington. These production reactors were used to produce plutonium for nuclear weapons. The Hanford reactors were complex systems that required the collaboration of a large number of traditional engineers from all disciplines. The team also

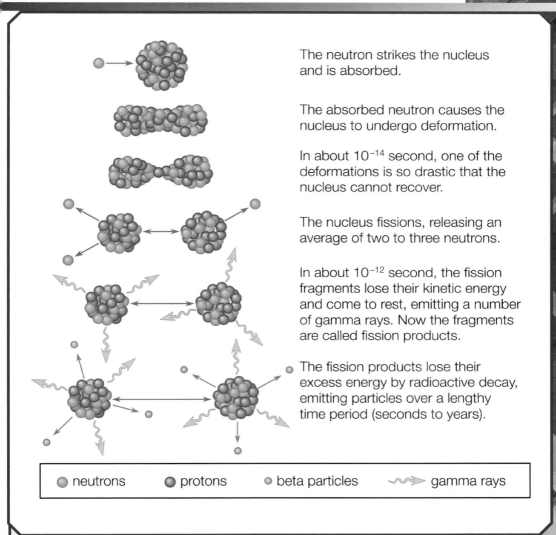

The neutron strikes the nucleus and is absorbed.

The absorbed neutron causes the nucleus to undergo deformation.

In about 10^{-14} second, one of the deformations is so drastic that the nucleus cannot recover.

The nucleus fissions, releasing an average of two to three neutrons.

In about 10^{-12} second, the fission fragments lose their kinetic energy and come to rest, emitting a number of gamma rays. Now the fragments are called fission products.

The fission products lose their excess energy by radioactive decay, emitting particles over a lengthy time period (seconds to years).

neutrons   protons   beta particles   gamma rays

This diagram illustrates the sequence of events in the fission of a uranium nucleus by a neutron. This is the basis of nuclear engineering.

included physicists and mathematicians who could work with the engineers to design and analyze early reactor systems. These

physicist-mathematician-engineers were the ancestors of today's nuclear engineers.

The successful development of nuclear submarines by the U.S. Navy after World War II was a key driver for the then-unnamed discipline of nuclear engineering. The design and analysis of nuclear reactors, whether on land or in a submarine, requires an understanding of the complex nuclear phenomena going on within the reactors as well as a practical knowledge of how to design and build the fuel assemblies, cooling systems, pressure vessels, control systems, and other systems needed for the reactor plant. A growing understanding of nuclear physics within the reactor and of radiation transport within and outside the reactor led to the birth of a new engineering discipline, nuclear engineering, that supplemented the traditional (and necessary) engineering disciplines needed to design, analyze, build, and operate a nuclear reactor plant.

In the late 1940s and early 1950s, as the many potential peaceful uses of nuclear energy became evident, schools of reactor technology were established by Oak Ridge National Laboratory in Tennessee and by Argonne National Laboratory near Chicago. These schools were the forerunners of the first academic departments and degree programs established in the 1950s and '60s by colleges and universities around the United States, including North Carolina State University, Pennsylvania State University, and the University of Michigan.

The successful application of nuclear reactors to naval propulsion led directly to the rapid development of commercial nuclear power plants in the 1960s and '70s. This in turn increased demand for nuclear engineers. Today there are more than 40 departments and programs offering courses in nuclear engineering and related fields in the United States and

Nuclear engineers are critical to the functioning of nuclear power plants, which derive their heat from fission in a nuclear reactor.

Canada, and more than sixty such programs have been established elsewhere in the world.

While the primary driver for the growth of nuclear engineering has been nuclear power, the discipline has broader applications. Nuclear engineering also includes fields such as radiation measurement and imaging, nuclear fusion and plasma physics, nuclear materials, and medical and health physics. In order to represent this broader spectrum of activities, some nuclear engineering departments have expanded their titles to include "nuclear science," "radiological sciences," or "radiation sciences."

BIOENGINEERING

Before World War II, the field of bioengineering was essentially unknown, and little communication or interaction existed between the engineer and the life scientist. A few exceptions, however, should be noted. The agricultural engineer and the chemical engineer, involved in fermentation processes, have always been bioengineers in the broadest sense since they deal with biological systems. Mechanical engineers have worked with the medical profession for many years in the development of artificial limbs.

Today interaction between biology and engineering has greatly expanded, particularly in the medical and life-support fields. Much of the increase in bioengineering activity can be credited to electrical engineers. In the 1950s bioengineering meetings were dominated by sessions devoted to medical electronics.

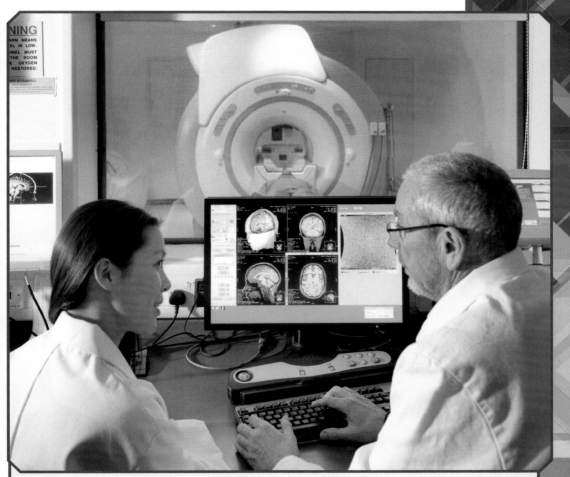

Although medical equipment and instruments, including imaging technology like the machine seen here, remain a focus of bioengineers, the field continues to expand to study other areas, including biomaterials and biological modeling.

Though medical instrumentation and medical electronics continue to be of importance, other areas of interest include biological modeling, blood-flow dynamics, prosthetics, biomechanics, biological heat transfer, and biomaterials.

Bioengineering developed out of specific desires or needs: the desire to make the blood's circulation bypass the heart during surgery; the need for replacement organs; the requirement for life support in space; and many more. In most cases the early interaction and education were a result of personal contacts between physician, or physiologist, and engineer.

Communication between the engineer and the life scientist was immediately recognized as a problem, however. Most engineers who wandered into the field in its early days probably were exposed to biology through a high-school course and no further work. To overcome this problem, engineers began to study not only the subject matter but also the methods and techniques of their counterparts in medicine, physiology, psychology, and biology. Much of the information was self-taught or obtained through personal association and discussions. Finally, recognizing a need to assist in overcoming the communication barrier as well as to prepare engineers for the future, engineering schools developed courses and curricula in bioengineering.

Industrial Engineering

Industrial engineering originated with the studies of Frederick W. Taylor, the Gilbreths, and other pioneers of mass production methods. Their work expanded into responsibilities that now include the development of work methods to increase efficiency and eliminate worker fatigue; the redesign and standardization of manufacturing processes and methods for handling and transporting materials; the development of production planning and control procedures; and the determination and maintenance of output standards for workers and machines. Today the field is characterized by an emphasis on mathematical and computer modeling.

In recent years industrial engineering has broadened significantly as a discipline. The support it now provides to production and manufacturing managers comes from specialists drawn from the field of industrial engineering and from operations research, management science, computer science, and information systems. In the 1970s and '80s industrial engineering became a more quantitative and computer-based profession, and operations research techniques were adopted

as the core of most industrial engineering academic curricula in both the United States and Europe.

Many problems of operations research originate in industrial production systems. It is often difficult to determine where the engineering discipline ends and the more basic scientific discipline begins (operations research is a branch of applied mathematics). Many academic departments now use the term *industrial engineering and operations research* or the reverse, further clouding the distinction.

AERONAUTICAL ENGINEERING

A major boost to aircraft development came during World War I, when aircraft were designed and constructed for specific military missions. The end of the war marked the decline of military high-technology aircraft and the rise of civil air transportation. Many advances in the civil sector were due to technologies gained in developing military and racing aircraft. It was the British who paved the way in civil aviation in 1920 with a twelve-passenger Handley-Page transport.

Aviation boomed after Charles A. Lindbergh's solo flight across the Atlantic

Ocean in 1927. Advances in metallurgy enabled aircraft to fly farther and faster. Hugo Junkers, a German, built the first all-metal monoplane in 1910, but the design was not accepted until 1933, when the Boeing 247-D entered service. The twin-engine design of the latter established the foundation of modern air transport.

The advent of the turbine-powered airplane dramatically changed the air transportation industry. Germany and Britain were concurrently developing the jet engine, but it was a German Heinkel He 178 that made the first jet flight on Aug. 27, 1939. Even though World War II accelerated the growth of the airplane, the jet aircraft was not introduced into service until 1944, when the British Gloster Meteor became operational, shortly followed by the German Me 262. The first practical American jet was the Lockheed F-80, which entered service in 1945.

Commercial aircraft after World War II continued to use the more economical propeller method of propulsion. The efficiency of the jet engine was increased, and in 1949 the British de Havilland Comet inaugurated commercial jet transport flight. The Comet, however, experienced structural failures that curtailed the service, and it was not until 1958 that the highly successful Boeing 707

THE RISE OF AEROSPACE ENGINEERING

The use of rocket engines for aircraft propulsion opened a new realm of flight to the aeronautical engineer. Robert H. Goddard, an American, developed, built, and flew the first successful liquid-propellant rocket on March 16, 1926. Goddard proved that flight was possible at speeds greater than the speed of sound and that rockets can work in a vacuum. The major impetus in rocket development came in 1938 when the American James Hart Wyld designed, built, and tested the first U.S. regeneratively cooled liquid

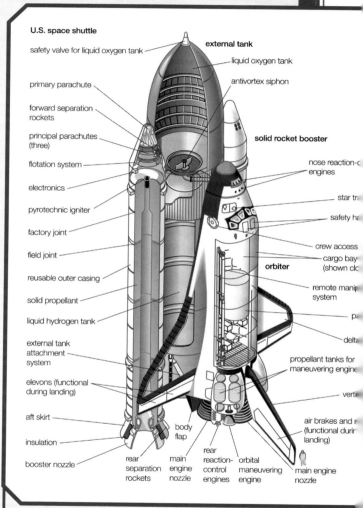

U.S. space shuttle

safety valve for liquid oxygen tank

primary parachute

forward separation rockets

principal parachutes (three)

flotation system

electronics

pyrotechnic igniter

factory joint

field joint

reusable outer casing

solid propellant

liquid hydrogen tank

external tank attachment system

elevons (functional during landing)

aft skirt

insulation

booster nozzle

external tank

liquid oxygen tank

antivortex siphon

solid rocket booster

nose reaction-c
engines

star tra

safety ha

crew access

cargo bay
(shown clc

orbiter

remote manip
system

pa

delta

propellant tanks for
maneuvering engine

verti

air brakes and r
(functional durir
landing)

body
flap

rear
separation
rockets

main
engine
nozzle

rear
reaction-
control
engines

orbital
maneuvering
engine

main engine
nozzle

This U.S. space shuttle is composed of a winged orbiter, an external liquid-propellant tank, and two solid-fuel rocket boosters.

rocket engine. In 1947 Wyld's rocket engine powered the first supersonic research aircraft, the Bell X-1, flown by U.S. Air Force captain Charles E. Yeager. Supersonic flight offered new challenges. The experience gained in the X-1 tests led to development of the X-15 research rocket plane, which flew nearly 200 flights over a nine-year period. The X-15 established an extensive database in transonic and supersonic flight (up to five times the speed of sound) and revealed vital information concerning the upper atmosphere.

The late 1950s and '60s marked a period of intense growth for astronautical engineering. In 1957 the U.S.S.R. orbited *Sputnik I*, the world's first artificial satellite, which triggered a space exploration race with the United States. In 1961 U.S. president John F. Kennedy asked Congress to undertake the challenge of "landing a man on the Moon and returning him safely to the Earth" by the end of the 1960s. This commitment was fulfilled on July 20, 1969, when astronauts Neil A. Armstrong and Edwin E. Aldrin, Jr., landed on the moon.

The 1970s began the decline of the U.S. manned spaceflights. The exploration of the Moon was replaced by unmanned voyages to Jupiter, Saturn, and other planets. The exploitation of space was redirected from conquering distant planets to providing a better understanding of the human environment. Artificial satellites provide data pertaining to geographic formations, oceanic and atmospheric movements, and worldwide communications. The frequency of U.S. spaceflights in the 1960s and '70s led to development of a reusable, manned space shuttle. Known officially as the Space Transportation System, the shuttle program flew 135 flights between its initial launch on April 12, 1981, and its final launch in 2011.

The British de Havilland Comet, seen here on display in 1949, was the precursor of the Boeing 707, which inaugurated transatlantic jet flight.

introduced the era of nonstop transatlantic jet transport.

Technological improvements in propulsion, materials, avionics, and stability and controls have enabled aircraft to grow in size, carrying more cargo faster and over longer distances. While aircraft are becoming safer and more efficient, they are also now very complex. Today's commercial aircraft are among the most sophisticated engineering achievements of the day.

CHAPTER 5

THE FUTURE OF ENGINEERING

Nearly all fields of engineering show signs of enduring well into the future and yielding significant advances that will undoubtedly impact life around the world. The frontiers being explored in two fields in particular—genetic engineering and environmental engineering—are especially promising. Successes in these fields have the potential to revolutionize health, medicine, quality of life, and much more.

GENETIC ENGINEERING

Genetic engineering had its origins during the late 1960s in experiments with bacteria, viruses, and plasmids, small, free-floating rings of DNA found in bacteria. A key discovery was made by Swiss microbiologist Werner Arber, who in 1968 discovered restriction enzymes. These are naturally occurring enzymes that cut DNA into fragments during replication.

A year later American biologist Hamilton O. Smith revealed that one type of restriction enzyme cut DNA at very specific points in the molecule. This enzyme was named type II restriction enzyme to distinguish it from type I and type III enzymes, which cut DNA in a different manner. In the early 1970s American biologist Daniel Nathans demonstrated that type II enzymes could be used to manipulate genes for research. For their efforts, Smith, Nathans, and Arber were awarded the 1978 Nobel Prize for Physiology or Medicine.

The true fathers of genetic engineering were American biochemists Stanley Cohen and Herbert Boyer, who were the first scientists to use restriction enzymes to produce a genetically modified organism. In 1973 they used type II enzymes to cut DNA into fragments, recombine the fragments in vitro, and then insert the foreign genes into a common laboratory strain of bacteria. The foreign genes replicated along with the bacteria's genome; furthermore, the modified bacteria produced the proteins specified by the foreign DNA.

Through recombinant-DNA techniques such as the one described, bacteria have been modified to synthesize human insulin, human interferon, human growth hormone, a

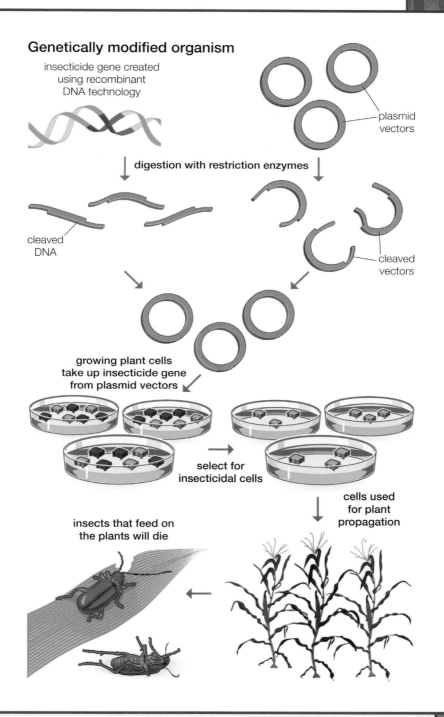

Genetically modified organism

insecticide gene created using recombinant DNA technology

plasmid vectors

digestion with restriction enzymes

cleaved DNA

cleaved vectors

growing plant cells take up insecticide gene from plasmid vectors

select for insecticidal cells

cells used for plant propagation

insects that feed on the plants will die

Genetically modified organisms are produced using scientific methods that include recombinant DNA technology.

WERNER ARBER

Swiss microbiologist Werner Arber received the 1978 Nobel Prize for Physiology or Medicine for finding a new method to study DNA, the molecules that convey genetic information. He discovered and used restriction enzymes, which break DNA molecules into units that are small enough to study separately but still large enough to carry meaningful information. Arber used restriction enzymes to study how organisms exchange genetic material and how bacteriophages, or viruses that infect bacteria, cause mutations in the bacteria they infect.

Arber was born on June 3, 1929, in Gränichen, Aargau canton (state), Switzerland. He attended Gränichen public schools and the Aarau Gymnasium (secondary school). From 1949 to 1953 he studied natural sciences at the Swiss Polytechnical School at Zürich.

In November 1953 Arber began a postgraduate assistantship

Werner Arber poses in 2003 at a BioVision forum in Lyon, France.

at the University of Geneva, Switzerland. His main responsibility was to care for two electron microscopes in the biophysics laboratory. While there, Arber learned about the genetics of bacteriophages and studied James Watson's and Francis Crick's groundbreaking research on the structure of DNA. Arber completed his doctorate in 1958.

After a year and a half in the United States at the University of Southern California, the University of California at Berkeley, Stanford, and Massachusetts Institute of Technology, Arber joined the University of Geneva faculty in 1960 with a focus on molecular genetics. After spending 1970–71 on a visiting appointment at Berkeley in molecular biology, he took up his new post as university professor in Basel, a Swiss city with a long tradition of industries related to biomedical research. He shared the Nobel Prize in 1978 with American scientists Daniel Nathans and Hamilton O. Smith.

hepatitis-B vaccine, and other medically useful substances. Recombinant-DNA techniques, combined with the development of a technique for producing antibodies in great quantity, have made an impact on medical diagnosis and cancer research. Plants have been genetically adjusted to perform nitrogen fixation and to produce their own pesticides. Bacteria capable

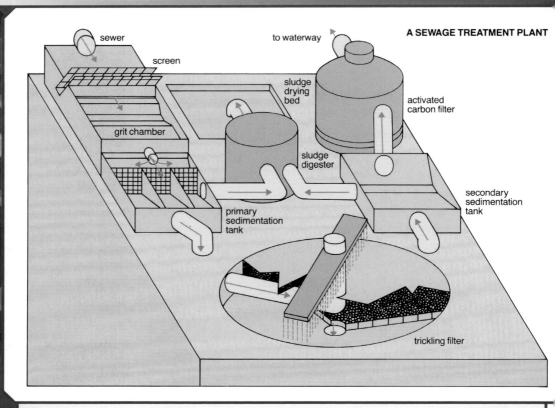

A SEWAGE TREATMENT PLANT

sewer

screen

to waterway

grit chamber

sludge drying bed

sludge digester

activated carbon filter

primary sedimentation tank

secondary sedimentation tank

trickling filter

Sewage treatment is one of many focuses of the environmental engineer. Knowledge of civil engineering, chemical engineering, and other fields may be useful to the environmental engineer as well.

of biodegrading oil have been produced for use in oil-spill cleanups.

In addition to its potential for positive change, however, genetic engineering also introduces the fear of adverse genetic manipulations and serious consequences, such as development of antibiotic-resistant bacteria or new strains of pathogenic, or disease-causing, bacteria.

ENVIRONMENTAL ENGINEERING

Environmental engineering is a field of broad scope that draws on such disciplines as chemistry, ecology, geology, hydraulics, hydrology, microbiology, economics, and mathematics. It was traditionally a specialized field within civil engineering and was called sanitary engineering until the mid-1960s, when the more accurate name environmental engineering was adopted.

Many of the products of mechanical engineering, together with technological developments in other fields, give rise to noise, the pollution of water and air, and the degradation of land and scenery. The rate of production, both of goods and power, is rising so rapidly that regeneration of resources by natural forces can no longer keep pace. Projects in environmental engineering involve the treatment and distribution of drinking water; the collection, treatment, and disposal of wastewater; the control of air pollution and noise pollution; municipal solid-waste management and hazardous-waste management; the cleanup of hazardous-waste sites; and the preparation of environmental assessments, audits, and impact studies. Mathematical modeling

and computer analysis are widely used to evaluate and design the systems required for such tasks. Chemical and mechanical engineers may also be involved in the process. Environmental engineering functions include applied research and teaching; project planning and management; the design, construction, and operation of facilities; the sale and marketing of environmental-control equipment; and the enforcement of environmental standards and regulations.

CONCLUSION

The history of engineering and technology is longer than and distinct from the history of science. Engineering is the systematic study of techniques for making and doing things; science is the systematic attempt to understand and interpret the world. While technology is concerned with the fabrication and use of artifacts, science is devoted to the more conceptual enterprise of understanding the environment, and it depends upon the comparatively sophisticated skills of literacy and numeracy. Throughout time, however, science and technology, by way of engineering, have become deeply intertwined. Technology has created new tools and machines with which the scientists have been able to achieve an ever-increasing insight into the natural world.

The role of Thomas Edison is particularly significant in the deepening relationship between science and technology, because the prodigious trial-and-error process by which he selected the carbon filament for his electric lightbulb in 1879 resulted in the creation at Menlo Park, N.J., of what may be regarded as the world's first genuine industrial research laboratory. From this achievement the application of scientific principles to technology grew rapidly. It led easily to the engineering rationalism applied by Frederick W. Taylor to the organization of workers in mass production. It provided a model that was applied rigorously by Henry Ford in his automobile assembly plant and that was followed by every modern mass-production process. It pointed the way to the development of systems engineering, operations research, simulation studies, mathematical modeling, and technological assessment in industrial processes. Taken together, these developments have brought technology to its modern highly efficient level of performance and continue to promise unprecedented innovation and societal advancement.

aerodynamics A branch of dynamics that deals with the motion of air and other gaseous fluids and with forces acting on bodies in motion relative to such fluids.

avionics Electronics designed for use in aerospace vehicles.

distillation The process of purifying a liquid by successive evaporation and condensation.

draftsmanship The skill of making drawings that will be used to make machines, buildings, or other structures.

efficiency The ratio of the useful energy delivered by a dynamic system to the energy supplied to it.

fluid mechanics The science concerned with the response of fluids to forces exerted upon them.

hydraulic Operated by the resistance offered or the pressure transmitted when a quantity of liquid (as water or oil) is forced through a comparatively small orifice or through a tube.

hydroelectric Of or relating to the production of electricity by using machines that are powered by moving water.

metallurgy The art and science of extracting metals from their ores and modifying the metals for use.

nuclear fission The splitting of an atomic nucleus resulting in the release of large amounts of energy.

ozone A very reactive form of oxygen that is a bluish irritating gas of pungent odor and that is formed naturally in the atmosphere by a photochemical reaction; a major air pollutant in the lower atmosphere but a beneficial component of the upper atmosphere, and used for oxidizing, bleaching, disinfecting, and deodorizing.

polymer A chemical compound or mixture of compounds formed by polymerization and consisting essentially of repeating structural units.

prosthetics The surgical or dental specialty concerned with the design, construction, and fitting of artificial devices that replace a missing or injured part of the body.

recombinant DNA Genetically engineered DNA usually incorporating DNA from more than one species.

supersonic Faster than the speed of sound.

thermodynamics Science of the relationship between heat, work, temperature, and energy. In broad terms, thermody-namics deals with the transfer of energy from one place to another and from one form to another. The key concept is that heat is a form of energy corresponding to a definite amount of mechanical work.

turbine A rotary engine triggered by the reaction or impulse or both of a current of fluid (as water, steam, or air) subject to pressure and usually made with a series of curved vanes on a central rotating spindle.

work The energy that is produced when a force is applied over a given distance. Work is done when a force is applied to an object and the object is moved over a given distance.

American Society for Engineering
   Education (ASEE)
1818 N Street NW, Suite 600
Washington, DC 20036
(202) 331-3500
Website: http://www.asee.org
The American Society for Engineering
   Education is dedicated to advancing
   engineering education for all students
   through research, leadership, and a
   variety of services. The organization's
   activities include curriculum development, workshops, and conferences.

The Bakken Museum
3537 Zenith Avenue South
Minneapolis, MN 55416
(612) 926-3878
Website: http://thebakken.org
The Bakken Museum is dedicated to pro-
   moting public interest in electricity and
   magnetism. In addition to its interac-
   tive exhibits, the museum has a variety
   of programs for students interested in
   building and inventing.

Canadian Society of/for Professional
　　Engineers (CSPE)
4950 Yonge Street, Suite 502
Toronto, ON M2N 6K1
Canada
(416) 223-9961
Website: http://www.cspe.ca/CSPE/Main_
　　Page.html
The CSPE advocates for professional engi-
　　neers in Canada, seeking to address
　　professional concerns, such as licensing
　　and regulation in the industry.

Engineering Is Elementary (EIE)
Museum of Science
1 Science Park
Boston, MA 02114
(617) 589-0230
Website: http://www.eie.org
The Engineering Is Elementary pro-
　　gram, part of the National Center for
　　Technological Literacy at the Museum of
　　Science, encourages engineering literacy
　　for students of all ages. The program
　　offers various curriculum materials online
　　and other resources, such as workshops,
　　at the museum.

FIRST
200 Bedford Street
Manchester, NH 03101
(800) 871-8326
Website: http://www.usfirst.org
FIRST fosters curiosity and engagement
    with science and technology among young
    people by sponsoring various programs
    and competitions. Different programs for
    different age ranges allow participants to
    develop a hands-on approach to innovation
    in robotics and technology.

National Society of Professional Engineers
    (NSPE)
1420 King Street
Alexandria, VA 22314
(888) 285-6773
Website: http://www.nspe.org
The NSPE serves the non-technical con-
    cerns of professional engineers. The
    organization offers educational services
    and other resources to those looking to
    obtain a license and ensures the value of
    licensure for already licensed engineers.

NYLF: Explore STEM
Envision
1101 Pennsylvania Avenue NW, Suite 600

Washington, DC 20004

(703) 584-9513

Website: http://www.envisionexperi-
ence.com/explore-our-programs/
nylf-explore-stem#what-to-expect

The Explore STEM program of the National
Youth Leadership Forum (NYLF) offers
a summer camp each year to students
interested in pursuing careers in science,
technology, engineering, and math. The
camp offers students an opportunity to
interact with leaders in STEM fields,
participate in hands-on projects and
workshops, and make field visits.

Society for Canadian Women in Science and
Technology (SCWIST)

311–525 Seymour Street

Vancouver, BC V6B 3H7

Canada

(607) 893-8657

Website: http://www.scwist.ca

SCWIST supports women and girls engaged
in science- and technology-related fields
or studies. The organization inspires students to pursue STEM careers through
conferences, workshops, and various
programs. Professional resources are also
offered.

Society of Women Engineers (SWE)
203 N. LaSalle Street, Suite 1675
Chicago, IL 60601
(877) 793-4636
Website: http://societyofwomenengineers.
    swe.org
SWE provides a voice for women engi-
    neers and helps advance their role and
    image in the engineering industry. The
    organization also offers resources to
    K–12 students interested in pursuing an
    engineering education.

WEBSITES

Because of the changing nature of Internet
links, Rosen Publishing has developed an
online list of websites related to the subject
of this book. This site is updated regularly.
Please use this link to access this list:

http://www.rosenlinks.com/SCI/Eng

Baine, Celeste. *Is There an Engineer Inside You?: A Comprehensive Guide to Career Decisions in Engineering*. Springfield, OR: Bonamy Publishing, 2013.

Blockley, David. *Engineering: A Very Short Introduction*. New York, NY: Oxford University Press, 2012.

Brain, Marshall. *The Engineering Book: From the Catapult to the Curiosity Rover, 250 Milestones in the History of Engineering*. New York, NY: Sterling, 2015.

Conway, Erik M. *Exploration and Engineering: The Jet Propulsion Laboratory and the Quest for Mars*. Baltimore, MD: Johns Hopkins University Press, 2015.

Goddard, Jolyon. *Concise History of Science & Invention: An Illustrated Time Line*. Washington, DC: National Geographic, 2009.

Hagler, Gina. *Top STEM Careers in Engineering*. New York, NY: Rosen, 2015.

Johnson, Michael Peter. *Mission Control: Inventing the Groundwork of Spaceflight*. Gainesville, FL: University Press of Florida, 2015.

Johnson, Steven. *How We Got to Now: Six Innovations that Made the Modern World.* New York, NY: Penguin, 2014.

Kemp, Adam. *The Makerspace Workbench: Tools, Technologies, and Techniques for Making.* Sebastopol, CA: Maker Media, 2013.

Lusted, Marcia Amidon. *Careers for Tech Girls in Engineering.* New York, NY: Rosen, 2016.

Miodownik, Mark. *Stuff Matters: Exploring the Marvelous Materials that Shape Our Man-Made World.* New York, NY: Houghton Mifflin Harcourt, 2014.

Platt, Charles. *Electronics: A Hands-On Primer for the New Electronics Enthusiast.* Sebastopol, CA: Maker Media, 2009.

Rice, Elizabeth. *Genetic Engineering.* New York, NY: Cavendish Square Publishing, 2014.

Wells, Matthew. *Engineering: A History of Engineering and Structural Design.* New York, NY: Routledge, 2010.